Copyright © 2022 Dr. Tia Palmer

All rights reserved. No part of this publication may be reproduced, distributed, or transmitted in any form or by any means, including photocopying, recording, or other electronic or mechanical methods, without the prior written permission of the publisher, except in the case of brief quotations embodied in critical reviews and certain other non-commercial uses permitted by copyright law.

IT'S JUST ALOPECIA

A STORY BY **DR. TIA PALMER**   ILLUSTRATED BY **DARICE POLLARD**

I have Alopecia. Alopecia is a skin condition that makes you lose your hair.

Even though I'm bald, I'm just a normal kid.

I like to run,

...play with my toys,

...and play on my tablet like other kids.

Sometimes I like to wear my cap,

...sometimes I don't because I'm handsome and my bald head is cool!

But don't rub it unless I give you permission.

Anyone can get alopecia, but it's more common in kids and young adults.

Boys and girls can have alopecia.

There are **147 MILLION** people in the **WORLD** like me,

who have or will have alopecia.

About **6.8 MILLION** of those people are in the United States.

That's like **1** in every **500** to **1,000** people.

My bald head makes me unique, but treat me like any other kid.

I'm not sick.
I don't have cancer.
It's not contagious...

www.ingramcontent.com/pod-product-compliance
Lightning Source LLC
LaVergne TN
LVHW071702060526
838201LV00038B/404